ANTONI

GAUDÍ

Author: Jeremy Roe
Layout:
Baseline Co. Ltd.
127-129A Nguyen Hue
Fiditourist Building, 3rd floor
District 1, Ho Chi Minh City
Vietnam

ISBN: 1-85995-924-5

Printed in Singapore

ANTONI
GAUDÍ

CONTENTS

Essential Gaudí

In order to understand the real significance of Gaudí's architecture it is necessary to take into account various factors which influenced his thinking. His family background, childhood, place of birth and schooling, the historical context of Catalonia and Spain during his lifetime, his friends and relations, all form the framework for the very special and very distinct architecture of Antoni Gaudí Cornet.

However, his personality is hard to capture for various reasons. In the first place, Gaudí's shy and retiring nature meant that there are virtually no original documents in existence that show what he was like. He closely guarded his privacy, and it is a *sancta sanctorum* into which the historian should not try to penetrate, both out of respect and because he lacks sufficient judgement to draw any definite conclusions.

Hence the numerous fantasies that have been written about Gaudí – fabrications that are of no historical value despite their appeal to the public, ever eager for details of the intimate lives of great men regardless of whether or not they are true. Gaudí's family background must be taken very much into account, for the nature of the trade which his father and both his paternal and maternal grandfathers followed is very revealing. More than five generations of Gaudís had been coppersmiths, producing the vats for distilling alcohol from the grapes grown in the Camp de Tarragona.

The spatial aspects of the curved forms of these vats, made of beaten copper plates, had a considerable influence on Gaudí, as he himself admitted, for they taught him to visualise bodies in space rather than projected geometrically on to a single plane. These visions from his childhood and his father's workshop of brightly coloured, shining, malleable shapes, sculptural living forms, persisted in his architecture.

Brought up in a Christian family of artisans and craftsmen, he went to school at the Piarist college in Reus, where he received a broad-minded and humanistic education that undoubtedly played and important part in defining his character. There he met Eduard Toda Güell, who sowed in him the seeds of a love of the monastery of Poblet and of the history of Catalonia in general.

The town of Reus in the middle of the nineteenth century was a centre of political, radical and republican agitation. Although Gaudí never left any desire to play an active part in politics, nor in anything else other than his own particular form of architecture, it is clear that he caught the strong feelings of those around him and became deeply concerned about the serious problems from which the country suffered.

He was a student during the last of the Carlist Wars, and although he never actually had to take part in any fighting he was mobilised for the entire duration.

When later, while studying architecture in Barcelona, he showed his concern for the problems of the working classes by collaborating in the design of *La Obrera Mataronense,* the first co-operative factory in Spain, he was putting into practice some of the ideas he had formed during his schooldays in Reus.

Reus and the nearby village of Riudoms, where he spent many summers in a small cottage that his father owned, both had an influence on Gaudí, not only through the character of their inhabitants but also through their climate and landscape.

Dry stony lands, with a special luminosity, where vines, almonds, hazels, cypresses, carobs, pines and olives grew: lands that could have been set in Lazio or the Peloponnese; Mediterranean lands *par excellence*, which Gaudí considered the ideal place in which to contemplate Nature, for the sun shines with unusual splendour and falls on the ground at an angle of forty-five degrees, producing the most perfect light effects. Reality in all its truth and beauty could be found in the landscape of the Camp de Tarragona under the Mediterranean sun.

Gaudí considered himself an observer of things in their natural state. His immense imagination was based only on the capacity to assimilate the reality of Nature, exquisitely lit and portrayed by the sun of that beautiful region. But we all know that the sun - including the sun in the Camp de Tarragona- shines for everyone, but it does not suggest to everyone what it suggested to Gaudí. And this brings us to a second factor, for Gaudí's capacity for observation was a result of his being a sickly child who suffered from rheumatic fever, which prevented him from joining in the games the other children played. Isolated and alone, he spent the best part of his time observing Nature, and he realised, with intelligent perception, that of the infinite number of forms that exist in the world, some are highly suitable for structures whilst others are highly suitable for decoration.

At the same time he noted that structure and decoration occur simultaneously in Nature - in plants, rocks and animals - and that Nature creates structural forms that are both statically perfect and extremely beautiful, and are based merely on functionality.

The structural part of a tree and the skeleton of a mammal do no more than strictly conform to the laws of gravity, and hence the laws of mechanics.

The scent and formal beauty of a flower are no more than the mechanisms for attracting insects and thus ensuring the reproduction of the species. Nature creates beautifully decorated structures without the slightest intention of creating works of art.

At this stage we must consider another point in relation to Gaudí's character. It has been explained how the concept of structure was formed in his mind from the beaten copper shapes that his father produced in his workshop. But among Gaudí's ancestors there were no architects or even bricklayers. This meant that he was not burdened with three thousand years of architectural culture, as occurs in families of architects.

Although the history of architecture has taken many turns, and seemingly very different styles have followed each other in succession, in actual fact from the early Egyptians to the present day the architecture of architects has been based on simple geometry involving lines, two-dimensional figures and regular polyhedrons combined with spheres, ellipses and circles. This architecture was always produced from plans - plans which have always been produced with simple instruments like the compass and set square and from which the masons have always worked.

Gaudí, however, saw that Nature made to preliminary drawings and appeared to use none of these instruments for constructing its beautifully decorated structures. Moreover, Nature, whose field covers all forms of geometry, rarely uses the most simplified one which is common to the architects of all ages. Without any architectural preconceptions, but at the same time with great humility, he considered that there is nothing more logical than that which is created by Nature, with millions of years of trying out forms until they were perfected.

He tried, with much thought and reflection, to discover the geometry that could be used for architectural construction and that, in addition, had been habitually employed by Nature in plants and animals. His research covered both plane and solid geometry, but in order to follow more clearly his line of thinking the two will be dealt with separately here.

It is a well-known fact that the arch, as a development on the lintel rearranged in voussoirs, was used in the Ancient East and also by the Etruscans, who passed it on to the Romans. Arches in ancient architecture were basically semicircular, or else were segmental, elliptical or basket arches.

In Nature, when an arch forms spontaneous – on a mountain eroded by the wind, or due to rocks falls - it is never semicircular nor any other shape drawn by architects using a compass.

Natural arches are appreciably parabolic or catenary. Strangely enough, the catenary arch, which follows the curve formed by a chain suspended freely from two points, but inverted, and possesses excellent mechanical properties that were already known by the end of the seventeenth century, was scarcely ever used by architects, who considered it ugly, influenced as they were by long centuries of architectural tradition that had accustomed them to shapes drawn with a compass.

Gaudí on the other hand, thought that if this arch was the most mechanically perfect and was the one produced spontaneously by Nature, then it must be the most beautiful because it was the most simple and functional. Simple as regards its natural formation, but not when drawn with architectonic instruments.

In the stables at the *Finca Güell* (1884), the waterfall in the garden of the *Casa Vicens* (1883), in the blanching room at *La Obrera Mataronense* (1883), Gaudí used this type of arch with confidence and with supreme elegance, and he continued to employ it in his more modern buildings such as *Bellesguard* (1900), the *Casa Batlló* (1904) and *La Pedrera* (1906). With regard to solid geometry, he noticed the frequent occurrence in Nature of ruled warped surfaces - that is to say, curved surfaces generated solely by straight lines.

All natural forms of a fibrous composition, such as a cane, a bone or the tendons of muscles, will, when they are twisted or warped and the fibres remain straight, produce so-called ruled warped surfaces. A bundle of sticks dropped on the floor will form these warped surfaces, and the tents of the North American Indians are built of poles covered with skins which form ruled warped surfaces.

It was not until the end of the eighteenth century that these warped surfaces were studied geometrically (mainly by Gaspard Monge), and it was then that they were given the complicated names of helicoids, hyperbolic paraboloids, hyperboloids and conoids. The names are difficult, but the geometric forms are very easy to understand and to produce.

A hyperbolic paraboloid is formed by two straight lines, in different planes, with a third line sliding continuously along them, thus generating a curved figure in space which is formed entirely of straight lines.

Hyperbolic paraboloids can be found in mountain passes, between the fingers of one's hand, etc. The Indian wigwam referred to earlier is a hyperboloid, as is the human femur. The shoots on the stalk of a plant grow helicoidally, and the bark of eucalyptus trees is helicoidal.

Geometry generated by straight lines can be found in all the kingdoms of

Nature (animal, vegetable and mineral) and it produces forms that are structurally perfect.

Gaudí noticed something else. In Catalonia, a system of construction that has long been and still is frequently used is one that consists in laying slim bricks so that only the largest face is visible (the bricks in each course being laid end to end). This process, using plaster, lime mortar or cement for the joints and forming surfaces one or two layers thick, is employed for floors, partitions or walls and also for vaults, which are warped surfaces in space and are known in Catalan as *voltes de maó de pla*. To construct these, bricklayers generally use flexible wooden battens, although sometimes they simply make do with two rules and a string, and the results can be seen in lofty staircases and ceilings.

Gaudí thought that if one started with two rules on different planes and built the various courses of the vault following the string running from rule to rule, one would obtain a perfect hyperbolic paraboloid. He thus found, in this traditional Catalan method of construction, the opportunity to produce ruled warped forms very similar to those encountered in Nature, pleasing to the eye and with excellent load-bearing capacities.

He achieved the same shining curved forms that his father had produced by beating cooper in his workshop – except that Gaudí used bricks laid in straight lines and then covered them with chips of tiles (*trencadís*, in Catalan) to give a shiny, iridescent effect.

His architecture was conceived in the coppersmith's workshop, the result of his ingenuous but intelligent observation of the ruled warped surfaces of Nature and of the delightfully simple Catalan technique of building shallow vaults. It has nothing in common with the elaborate and repetitive architecture of history, rooted as it is in Euclidean geometry.

The architecture of architects came to a standstill when it began to be studied from the historical point of view. The history of architecture led to historicism, and things became even more complicated with the advent of the study of treatises on architecture. All this has produced a science of science, overloading architecture with theories and philosophical concepts that end by taking it further and further from reality.

Gaudí started to play the game of architecture from scratch; he changed the current geometry by replacing cubes, spheres and prisms with hyperboloids, helicoids and conoids, decorating them with natural features such as flowers, water or rocks. He changed the basis of architecture – which is geometry – and thus completely changed the state of the art.
The result was spectacular, but although admired by many it was little understood by the majority. This is why his style of architecture has been described as confused, chaotic, surrealist or degenerate. Those who think or say this are unaware that Gaudí's architecture is based on the geometry of Nature and on traditional methods of construction.

It is clear that Gaudí used forms that had never been seen in building before, and that he never repeated any of the immense variety of features that made up his repertory; but the surprising thing is that he achieved all this by means of the most ordinary and traditional methods of construction.

He never made use of modern building inventions, or reinforced concrete, or huge steel structures, or even new materials. With these new materials it is, to some extent, obvious that new forms can be achieved, but to produce something new with old-fashioned techniques is a sign of brilliance.

This architecture that is seemingly complicated but is in fact as simple as Nature, the master of logic, arose from the hands of Gaudí like a sculpture formed of ruled warped surfaces, structurally perfect but at the same time markedly organic, alive and pulsating.

Anyone who has visited the chapel at the *Colònia Güell in Santa Coloma de Cervelló* (1908-15) will have felt himself inside a living, breathing structure that produces a sensation of muscular tension, with walls like a skin that must surely be warm, as if the blood coursed strongly beneath it.

Gaudí, who was brought up in the Camp de Tarragona and whose buildings are located mainly in Barcelona, expressed his Mediterranean and Catalan spirit by showing the world that there is another way, another geometry, that can produce an architecture more in tune with Nature.

It is an architecture that is logical, clear and as transparent as the light in the Alt Camp; an architecture that is not abstract but very concrete, that invents nothing but rather goes back to origins, as he once explained in his famous phrase: "Originality means returning to the origin of things."

Gaudí not only saw these origins in the natural things of this world, but he also embellished and idealised them with religious feeling derived from the simple precept of St. Francis of Assisi, who loved Nature because it was the work of the Creator.

Prof. Dr. Arch. Juan Bassegoda Nonell, Hon. FAIA
Curator of the Gaudí Chair, Barcelona

Perspectives on the Life of Antoni Gaudí

The life of Antoni Gaudí (1852-1926) is best told and analysed through a focused study of his works. The buildings, plans and designs testify to Gaudí's character, interests and remarkable creativity in a way that research into his childhood, his daily routines and working habits can illuminate only dimly.

In addition to this, Gaudí was not an academic thinker keen to preserve his thoughts and ideas for posterity through either teaching or writing. He worked in the sphere of practical, rather than theoretical work. Were this not enough to challenge attempts to gauge the mind of this innovative architect the violence of Spain's Civil War resulted in the destruction of a large part of the Gaudí archive, and this has denied a deeper understanding of Gaudí the man, his character and thoughts. On 29* July in the first year of the Spanish Civil war the *Sagrada Familia* was broken into, and documents, designs and architectural models stored in the crypt were destroyed.

The absence of documentation limits the possibility of a searching biographical study, and it has encouraged rather more speculative interpretations of the architect. Today Gaudí has gained an almost mythic status in the same way that his buildings have become iconic. While his work continues to attract the 'devotions' of many thousands of tourists, his life inspires a range of responses. Besides the academic scholarship of Juan Bassegoda Nonell, for example, or the recent biographical study of Gijs Van Hensenberg, the life of Gaudí has prompted hagiographies and more imaginative reflections. In a different vein Barcelona's acclaimed opera house, el Liceu, premiered the opera *Antoni Gaudí* by Joan Guinjoan in 2004 and this process of cultural celebration has taken on a metaphysical dimension with the campaign by the Associació Pro Beataifició d'Antoni Gaudí to canonise him.

The ongoing celebrations and constructions of Gaudí the man by various groups signals how in our 'Post-Modern' age the ascetic, inspired, untiring creator remains a key trope of creativity in the popular imagination. Gaudí remains an enigmatic figure and attempts to interpret him tend to tell us more about the interpreter, as is illustrated in the following quotations.

Salvador Dalí records an exchange with the architect Le Corbusier in his essay *As of the Terrifying and Edible Beauty of Modern-Style Architecture*. Dalí stated, "…that the last great genius of architecture was called Gaudí whose name in Catalan means 'enjoy'."

He comments that Le Corbusier's face signalled his disagreement but Dalí continued, arguing that "the enjoyment and desire [which] are characteristic of Catholicism and of the Mediterranean Gothic" were "reinvented and brought to their paroxysm by Gaudí". The notion of Gaudí and his architecture with which the Surrealist confronted the rational Modernist architect illustrates a recurring feature in the historiography of Gaudí, which is the concern to isolate Gaudí from the specific history of architecture and render him as a visionary genius.

Furthermore, Dalí's account aims to place Gaudí in a pre-history of Surrealism and identify Gaudí as a 'prophet' or precursor of the aesthetics and ideas of that avant-garde Modernist movement.

While the devout Catholic and studious architect Gaudí may have considered anathema much of Dalí's art and writing, he may not have disagreed entirely with Dalí's comments cited here.

However, it should be noted that to identify Gaudí as a proto-Surrealist risks obscuring Gaudí's intellectual position, as well as his traditional religious beliefs. Considered from an historiographical angle Dalí's statement suggests an insight into Gaudí's continued appeal into the early twenty-first century. It may be argued that the frequent reappropriation and 'reinvention' of past styles in contemporary art, fashion and design has helped shape the appeal for Gaudí's artistic reappropriations, what Dalí termed his "paroxysm of the Gothic".

It is of the utmost relevance to note that Le Corbusier was by no means antipathetic to Gaudí. In 1927 he is recorded as saying, "What I had seen in Barcelona was the work of a man of extraordinary force, faith, and technical capacity. . . Gaudí is 'the' constructor of 1900, the professional builder in stone, iron, or bricks. His glory is acknowledged today in his own country. Gaudí was a great artist. Only they remain and will endure who touch the sensitive hearts of men…"

As will become apparent, Gaudí would have probably shared Le Corbusier's sentiments more than Dalí's. Le Corbusier's criticism signals a different approach to the analysis of Gaudí's work. It is examined in the specific context of architectural history.

In the course of this book, analysis of Gaudí's buildings seeks to balance the measured architectural analysis evoked by Le Corbusier with discussion of the shifting critical responses to Gaudí's work such as Dalí's. The foundation for this approach is a critical understanding of Gaudí's life. His interests and the society of Barcelona, which shaped his work in important ways, need to be considered and they are the subjects to be treated. It needs to be emphasised that in the absence of further information it is the buildings which are the best testament to the man.

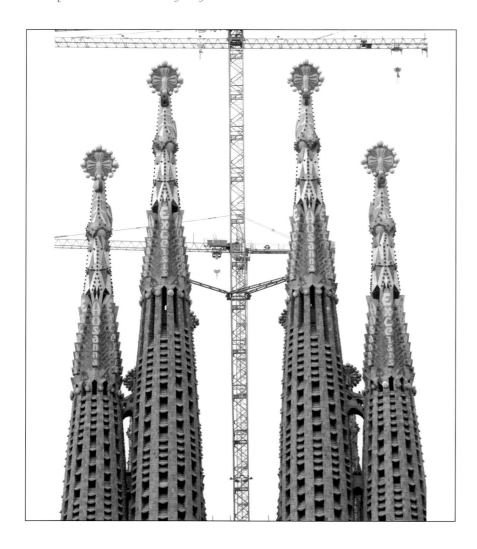

1. Park Güell, *trencadís* mosaïc of the bench.
2. Portrait of Gaudí
3. Temple of Sagrada Familia, New towers of the Nativity façade.
4. Episcopal Palace of Astorga, General view of façade.

Gaudí's Childhood

Gaudí was not born in Barcelona, the city that provided a key cultural dynamic to his architecture, but he was born in Catalonia, in the small town of Reus. Biographers of Gaudí, often prompted by the architect himself, have identified in his provincial childhood experiences the origins of his later creativity. The belief that art may be an inherited gift underpins Gaudí's assertion that his "quality of spatial apprehension" was inherited from the three generations of coppersmiths on his father's side of the family, as well as a mariner on his mother's side. Whatever truth there may be in Gaudí's claim, we can be certain that his home life was comfortable and stable. The only shadow cast over his childhood was a period of severe illness. The psychological effects of this on the development of the young child's imaginative faculties and spiritual convictions are hard to gauge, although his survival may be read as an early sign of a strong constitution and defiant determination.

It can be asserted with more confidence that this period of Gaudí's life introduced him to four factors that would be fundamental to his career: an interest in architecture, especially the Gothic; Catalan history and culture; Catholic doctrine and piety; and, finally, the forms and colours of the natural world.

In many ways architecture acted as a medium to explore and reflect on the latter three. Besides the traces of Reus's medieval heritage the neighbouring towns and countryside provided a number of important buildings to visit, such as the famed pilgrimage Church of Montserrat and Tarragona's impressive cathedral.

Gaudí's experiences of such places would have been coloured by an awareness of them as the cultural patrimony not of Spain, but the region of Catalonia, of which Barcelona is the capital. Catalonia had once been part of the independent Kingdom of Aragon, which first became linked to the Kingdom of Castile to form what we know as modern Spain in the fifteenth century. The process of balancing unification with regional autonomy is still being negotiated today and as a result Catalonia has developed a strong sense of national identity, with Barcelona at its centre.

The fact that many of the buildings Gaudí visited were religious is a reminder of the particular role that religion played in the construction of Catalan identity, as it did in the histories of other regions of Spain. As an adult, Gaudí would identify with both a defiant form of Catalan nationalism and a devout commitment to the Catholic Church. However, as a child and youth such serious concerns were a long way off.

Nonetheless, a keen youthful interest in architectural history and a concern for Catalan patrimony provided a foundation for his later ideological position. Besides visiting existing buildings Gaudí, accompanied by friends, would also seek out the ruins of once-great buildings and the traces of Catalonia's history. It would not seem fanciful to suggest that these excursions into the countryside inspired in Gaudí a creative vision of the landscape, stone, plants and other elements of the natural world. There is little verbal testimony of Gaudí's youthful attitudes to nature, and we must wait to examine his architecture to gauge this aspect of his thinking.

However, the clearest identification of the early signs of Gaudí's creative and intellectual powers are exemplified by an important episode from his youth, his involvement in a project to restore the ruined Cistercian monastery of Poblet.

In 1867, accompanied by his childhood friends Eduardo Toda and José Ribera Sans, Gaudí visited the ruins of the twelfth-century monastery. Documentary evidence of their visits records their imaginative impressions: the *Manuscrito de Poblet*, written by Toda in 1870, lists their plans to restore

the crumbling remains into an utopian cooperative, attracting the necessary labour force as well as a community of artists and writers, the combination of which would restore the monastery to a new life.

However, their youthful spirits were captured by the monastic ideal with art, life and pleasure as guiding principles, rather than by the restoration of Catholic tradition. It is worth noting that the *Manuscrito de Poblet* records the first known drawing by Gaudí of the heraldic shield of Poblet, which was produced in 1870.

In the 1930s Toda would return and lead the restoration of this monastery, but by that time Gaudí had been dead for four years. The intervening years had been spent by Gaudí not simply in imaginative restorations of the ruins, but in a creative and innovative interpretation of the architectural language of the past, as well as its values. It was as a student in Barcelona that this artistic process was initiated in earnest.

5. Finca Güell, Ladon, the guardian of the Gardens of the Hesperides (dragon detail).
6. Temple of Sagrada Familia, Sculptures on the old façade.

Gaudí's buildings for Güell illustrate the religious and utopian vision that the architect and his patron shared. The medieval world view evoked by Gaudí's work is also encountered in the allusions to palaces and castles of his domestic architecture for his wealthy patrons, the factory and the warehouse having become the modern fiefdoms. Although today discussion of such utopian ideals might appear naïve to modern visitors, their evocation in stone, space and light remains powerful. Another aspect of Gaudí's traditional outlook is noted in the way he organised his workshop with its many craftsmen. In addition to the emphasis placed on the use of manual skills, Gaudí maintained long working relationships with a range of architects such as Berenguer or Jujol, who both went on to become important independent architects in their own right.

As well as his equals in terms of education, Gaudí commanded respect from all of his team of assistants and he is recorded as being a strict but fair overseer. His paternalistic attitudes are noted for example in his encouragement of the workers not to drink alcohol and the allotting of lighter duties for the elder workers. A detailed study of the religious circles Gaudí frequented during his life remains to be undertaken. An additional association he was connected with was the *Cercle Artístic de Sant Lluc*. St Luke is the traditional patron saint of painters and this group, founded in 1894 by the sculptor Josep Lilmona, sought to promote Catholic art, as well as to counter the immoral avant-garde activities of Barcelona's *modernista* artists, such as Picasso. Gaudí became a member in 1899.

It is apparent that art was a fiercely contested space in Barcelona between those wanting to preserve tradition and their adversaries wanting to overthrow it. A number of caricatures explicitly parody Gaudí's religious beliefs, including a drawing by Picasso. In any case, a cautious approach is required to focus more closely on the relationships between Gaudí and Barcelona's Catholic intellectual fraternity.

Gaudí's famed individualism and his artistic vision mediated his contact with ideas. Firstly, he took his personal devotion very seriously, especially on reaching middle age. In 1894, during Lent, he subjected himself to a complete fast and was confined to bed. By then his fame as an architect was such that the local newspapers carried reports of his progress. In addition, accounts suggest that his conservative views could also be critical and his personal austerity, combined with his benevolent concern for the poor, prompted a critical stance of the Church.

Thus Gaudí's own independent thought serves to remind us that it was in his workshop with his architects and craftsmen that he designed, forged and carved his response to theology as well as to the nationalistic concerns of Catalan culture.

18. Temple of Sagrada Família,
Details of architectural decoration forms.

Gaudí's Death and Barcelona's Tributes to his Life

One way to measure Gaudí's public recognition is the response to his death. He was killed as a result of an accident. On Monday 7 June 1926, after a day's work in the workshop of the *Sagrada Familia*, he set off on foot, as was his custom, across the city to the Church of San Felipe Neri to attend confession. He was never to arrive. In the inquiry into his death the driver of a tram reported that he had hit a man who appeared to be a tramp, and that he had been unable to slow down.

The tramp-like figure was none other than Gaudí! After the accident he was assisted by two passers-by and the Guardia Civil, who eventually took him to a nearby dispensary. This after being refused assistance from several taxi drivers due to the appearance of the victim.

As a result of being knocked over by the tram Gaudí suffered fractured ribs, cerebral contusions and hemorrhaging in his ear. He was taken to hospital, yet he remained unidentified. The failure to identify Gaudí may be explained by the fact that his personal austerity had become such that he rarely changed his clothes, which were recognisable to his peers.

Although his appearance and clothes had been the subject of caricatures in the press, when seen in the grave context of a hospital and not set against the backdrop of the *Sagrada Familia*, his image rendered him anonymous.

However, Gaudí had not been forgotten. His friend Mossèn Gil Parés became concerned by his absence and that evening began looking for the architect in Barcelona's hospitals. He was found in the *Santa Cruz* hospital.

After he was recognised he was moved to a private room and the following day he regained consciousness. The news spread and Gaudí was visited by friends, official representatives of Church and State and others who wanted to show their respect for the architect.

As well as these displays of recognition for the man and his work, Gaudí's final days were also a display of his faith and political sentiments. He was given the sacrament of the Last Rites, and as he lay in bed awaiting death he held a crucifix. He had been offered a private clinic rather than the public hospital. Nevertheless he insisted that he remain and end his life amongst the people.

Gaudí died on Thursday 10 June. His passing was marked by a funeral that honoured his contribution to the traditions and faith of the Catalan people. Papal permission was acquired to bury him in the crypt of the *Sagrada Familia*, and the funeral took place on the Saturday.

The procession that followed his coffin to its final resting place testified to the architect's importance and recognition among the different areas of society: it included politicians from Barcelona as well as his native town of Reus; representatives of the Church; members of the religious and cultural associations to which he had belonged and to which he had contributed to, and many of the craftsmen from the city-workers' guilds also attended.

In this way the passion and commitment that Gaudí had shown in the different aspects of his life and work were all commemorated.

19. Güell Crypt, Stained glass window.

Gaudí's Barcelona

Gaudí and the Architecture of his Day

Gaudí's support for Catalan nationalism combined with his dedication to the Catholic faith, were important social and cultural factors that informed his work as an architect. These aspects of Gaudí's work can be examined in more detail, through an analysis of the development of a modern discourse and practice of architecture in Barcelona. Integral to these developments was Barcelona's national and spiritual identity. Both had evolved over the course of long histories spanning centuries, however in the nineteenth-century they were given renewed vigour and, what is more, became closely linked.

At the heart of this cultural change was the growing industrial strength and economic wealth of Barcelona and Catalonia as a whole. Architecture provided a key medium for individuals and the city to define a modern identity and express the new found optimism the modern era promised. This chapter locates Gaudí and his work amidst his contemporaries, and seeks to view him less as an isolated genius, instead as a man of his times whose work sought to embody many of the ideals of Barcelona as an historical, spiritual and modern city.

The following discussion combines discussion of historical and theoretical themes with an analysis of a series of works by Gaudí. Some of these are designs on paper and were never built or are now lost, while others are completed buildings. The intention is to provide a general introduction to Gaudí and Barcelona as the nineteenth-century merged into the twentieth, however it is also centred around the statement of Juan Bassegoda Nonell that,

> "When discussing Gaudí one cannot distinguish the concepts of
> architect, interior decorator, designer, painter or artisan. He was
> all of these things at the same time."

The works examined illustrate the diversity of Gaudí's skills, and although many of them could be called minor works they all offer fascinating insights into his design, art and architecture.

Gaudí may be identified with a number of artistic and intellectual currents running through Western Europe as industrialisation brought rapid change to almost all aspects of life. The *Arts and Crafts* Movement and the style known as Art Nouveau are the clearest parallels.

However, to map these webs of connections frequently offers a vision of the past configured more by contemporary interests. The approach taken here is to focus on the specific cultural setting of Barcelona, and in particular the movement known as *Modernisme*, which should be translated as Modernism with caution if at all, as it refers to a very specific period from around 1890 to 1910.

20. Casa Vicens, Tower detail.
21. Park Güell, Fountain.

Modernisme

*M*odernisme is applied to a range of visual and literary arts. With regard to architecture the term describes a group of architects led by Gaudí and Domènech i Montaner but also including other names such as Josep Marià Jujol, who worked closely with Gaudí. Where modern cultural movements begin and end is always a point of debate. Some historians would place the start of *Modernisme* between 1883 and 1888 with Gaudí's *Casa Vicens* while others not until Domènech's work for Barcelona's Universal Exhibition in 1888.

Consensus seems to have been reached that *Modernisme* as an architectural movement had run its course by 1910, which raises the issue of where to place Gaudí's last works such as the *Sagrada Familia*. Robert Hughes states:

"In certain respects Gaudí was not a *modernista* architect at all. His religious obsessions, for instance, separate him from the generally secular character of *Modernisme*. Gaudí did not believe in Modernity. He wanted to find radically new ways of being radically old..."

However, Gaudí may undoubtedly be identified as making a key contribution to Barcelona's *Modernisme*. To explore his identity as a 'modern figure' the concerns of *Modernisme* need to be considered in more detail. Attention will be focused firstly on the needs of the city, then on theories of architectural style and finally on the ideological dimensions of architecture.

22. Casa Vicens, Lateral façade.

Barcelona: The Growth of a Modern City

The history of nineteenth-century architecture in Barcelona is marked by a need to respond to the growth of the city. The rapid growth of population produced by industrial factories led to urban expansion beyond Barcelona's famed medieval quarter with its winding Gothic streets.

In 1859 the City Council held a competition for designs for a new urban plan. It was won by the engineer Ildefons Cerdà, who presented an abstract rational design of straight streets divided into equal blocks of living space, named the *Eixample*. At its heart were two diagonal avenues which intersected with a third horizontal one to create what is known today as the *Plaça de las Glòries Catalanes*.

In 1860 the first stone was laid by Queen Isabella II and Barcelona's appearance as a modern city was decided. Subsequent generations were critical of the design, for the lack of variety that it imposed on the city.

To maintain a focus on Gaudí it is not possible to consider in detail the merits or defects of Cerdà's plan; in any case it has subsequently been distorted by developers. Cerdà's plan had intended to integrate into the city important architectural features and social amenities to make urban life bearable, such as patio gardens at the heart of each block of apartments, centres for medical care and food markets. Cerdà's design was based in part on research of the existing living space of the city, and responded to the poverty that he saw.

While subsequent generations sought more imaginative solutions to the problem of urban space the design brief they were faced with was similar: to solve the social problems raised by changes to urban life.

Furthermore, Cerdà's *Eixample* established a standard type of townhouse with a façade facing the street, another looking onto a courtyard at the rear, and with load bearing walls built around patios that provided ventilation. The *Casa Batlló* and *Casa Milà* are Gaudí's contribution to Cerdà's plan and each are based on the type of house established by the *Eixample*.

Projects such as the Park Güell were also inspired by the aim to improve urban life, but in a less abstract way.

Finally, the scope of Cerdà's plan is a representative example of the new spirit that animated the minds of Barcelona's architects and patrons. While Gaudí and his contemporaries, the generation of *Modernisme*, thought very differently to Cerdà they all shared the confidence and vision to plan on a bold and grand scale.

23. Park Güell, Leaning columns of the viaducts.

24. Casa Milà, Façade from Calla Provença, balcony detail.
25. Casa Milà, Window detail view from the courtyard.

Theories of Architecture and the Search for a Modern Style

Cerdà's plans for the city were underpinned by his belief that, "... we lead a new way of life, functioning in a new way. Old cities are no more than an obstacle."

Considered in the context of nineteenth-century architecture his statement signals the distinction between an engineer and an architect.

For the architectural community the buildings of old cities, towns, and even ruins were an important source of inspiration for architectural style, which is a second factor informing *Modernisme*. Two currents of thought animated responses to the history of architecture: firstly, international developments in architectural theory and practice, and secondly, the development of a modern Catalan architecture.

Both of these formed an important foundation for Gaudí's development as an architect. The generation of his university teachers had been important in initiating this process. Elias Rogent i Amar was an architect whose work comprised both these elements. Unlike Gaudí, Rogent had travelled widely in Europe.

In addition to this he had studied the works of the French theorist Viollet-le-Duc, who is known for his important analysis of Gothic architecture, which concentrated not on its aesthetic appeal, but instead on the structural elements at its core.

The academic study of style in this French theorist's work provided a foundation for an increasingly eclectic use of architectural styles and decorative motifs. In Barcelona this eclecticism was frequently based on the use of regional Catalan styles, and often supplemented with other national Spanish styles such as the Moorish style.

An example of this gradual eclecticism in Rogent's work is found in the first major building added to Cerdà's *Eixample*.

In 1872, after twelve years of work, the new University of Barcelona was opened. On approaching the building there is little about the Romanesque style that declares itself as modern. However, no building from the Romanesque period exists on such a scale. The sober and ordered style places an emphasis on the horizontal plane created through the repetition of the arches on each storey. The rhythm created by the arches creates a harmonious effect and animates the imposing bare wall. The building evokes the form of a monastery: during the medieval period the monastic orders had made fundamental contributions to the establishment and the development of European universities. The choice of style is also concerned with origins. Catalonia is especially rich in Romanesque architecture and Rogent's choice was guided by an interest in employing a national style.

The nationalistic tendency in architectural practice would become well established, through the work of figures such as Rogent, by the time Gaudí began his studies.

However, it should be noted that the historical approach to style did not dictate the whole building: the interior decoration of Rogent's university building combines Islamic and Byzantine elements, and these clearly demonstrate eclecticism at work. Rogent's work and the ideas it upheld were a stage towards a more impassioned engagement with the modern and national significance of architecture, which the next generation took on.

In 1878, the year Gaudí qualified as an architect, a contemporary, Lluís Domènech i Montaner, published his essay "In Search of a National Architecture". Although a brief treatise, Domènech's essay provided an overview of the history of architectural style. Underpinning his analysis were the ideas of a second architectural theorist, Gottfried Semper, who in his writings had identified key structural elements fundamental to architecture and argued that style was dictated by social circumstances.

The lesson Domènech advocated was on the one hand the positive contribution of modern materials, and on the other a new approach to the lessons that could be learnt from history.

For Domènech the two ideas were inextricably linked, new materials provided new structural possibilities which in turn signified that the architecture of the past should not be slavishly imitated but, rather, applied to the new forms of architecture. Domènech's thesis marked a move away from the ideas of Rogent's generation, who adhered to an academic authenticity in their borrowings from the past, and Domènech initiated a new, bolder phase of eclecticism. Domènech fully recommended the study of all the history of architecture, "the practice of all good doctrines" but his aim was to, "... apply the forms that new experiences and needs impose on us, enriching them and giving them expressive strength," and he proudly declared himself guilty of eclecticism.

Gaudí would embrace his arguments, and the results bore impressive results in the houses he built, but in the last decades of his life he gradually developed his particular, mature style, which the architectural historian Mireia Freixa terms "the impossible confluence between abstraction and expression".

One of a number of Gaudí's statements, recorded by his disciples, illustrates his relationship to the ideas of Domènech, although when he said it is less certain:

"The aesthetic structure is that which explains the construction with its various resources and resolution of fecund problems, making pleasing objects for themselves… The first quality an object has to have in order to be beautiful is to achieve the aim for which it was intended…

In order that an object be beautiful in the highest sense it is necessary that its form has no superfluous detail, but that which is rendered useful to the material conditions."

Framed by the terms structure and beauty Gaudí offers his own theoretical insight into the themes raised by Domènech. Another comment ascribed to Gaudí clearly links him to eclecticism: "Originality is to return to the origin."

However, Gaudí's buildings often combined a number of origins and elements from Gothic, Romanesque and Moorish architecture. They are significant as they signal Domènech's identification of these styles as Spain's three national styles.

The two architects even worked together on a new design for the façade of the Barcelona Cathedral, which reveals their commitment to the development of a specific Catalan tradition. The ideological dimensions of their thinking provided an important dynamic in the development of their architectural work.

Architecture and Ideology

*M*ireia Freixa has written that, "The recovery of Catalan Culture is the task that unified the majority of Catalan artists and intellectuals in the broad period that runs from the *Renaixença* to *Noucentismo*. The *Modernista* generation simply substituted the romantic nostalgia for the decisive will to modernise the country..."

Freixa introduces two new terms, the *Renaixença* and *Noucentismo*, in addition to *Modernisme*. The second term is less relevant to the discussion of this chapter as it refers to the shift in interests from the more extravagant *Modernisme* to an austere classicism in the early twentieth-century.

However, the *Renaixença* is important. The term, which may be translated literally as 'the Renaissance', encompasses concerns to advance and protect the economic growth of Barcelona and Catalonia as well as to nourish the region's literary and artistic traditions.

Until the nineteenth century the economic and mercantile history of Barcelona has been one of periods of wealth and international recognition followed by decline.

During the course of the nineteenth century Catalonia, and Barcelona especially, witnessed a dramatic economic recovery as a centre for a range of industries and textiles, and from the wealth and confidence that resulted, the *Renaixença* was born.

Transforming Domestic Space

Apart from two remarkable country houses, Gaudí's secular and domestic architecture, surveyed in this chapter, is predominantly urban. Of these urban projects the majority were for Barcelona, and they are landmarks in the city's growth. All the buildings offer important perspectives on the social and cultural aspects of the Catalan *Renaixença*. Not only does this series of commissions document Gaudí's reflection on Catalan traditions of architecture, but they also serve as a testament to the economic development of Barcelona and a new class of wealthy patrons; it is interesting to note that a number of these houses combined offices and warehouse space for the commodities which their owners dealt in. To celebrate the strength of Catalan capital Gaudí looked to the past for paradigms of the region's strength and achievement, such as the renaissance palace or the medieval castle. Both provide a telling indication of the impression the owners wished to create.

Leaving the commissions for Eusebio Güell until later, this chapter traces the evolution of Gaudí's style through a focused study of some of Gaudí's

best known civic buildings, as well as many that are often overlooked. Two main themes are explored: firstly, Gaudí's creative engagement with the architectural vocabulary of past traditions, and secondly, his gradual development of radical and innovative approaches to a range of architectural tasks. The design of exterior façades, the creative use of interior space, the varied decorative methods and the imaginative effects achieved through subtle illumination are all examined.

Study of the following series of houses reveals how Gaudí first began to experiment with the contemporary 'rules' of architecture, which may be identified with the eclecticism of *Modernisme*. Then a second development emerges which shows how he sought to push his eclectic experiments further and almost reinvent the 'rules', as Gaudí developed a style that fused architectural tradition with a modern aesthetic based on nature and abstraction. The result of this process is a series of landmarks in 'modernist' architecture, which are crowned by the innovative *Casa Batlló* and *Casa Milà*.

36. Casa Vicens, View of façade from Calle de Carolines.
37. Casa Vicens, Detail of iron grille entrance.
38. Casa Vicens, Tower detail.

Casa Vicens

Gaudí's first domestic project was the *Casa Vicens*. Research in the municipal archives has found a signed plan for the house of 1883, but it is thought that Gaudí had begun preparing the designs as long as five years before. The lengthy planning process was matched by a long phase of construction. In 1888 the house was still awaiting completion. The complexity of Gaudí's design and the richness of the interior decoration account for the lengthy period of time he dedicated to this house. Although the *Casa Vicens* has undergone a number of changes it remains an impressive testament to Gaudí's skill at this early stage of his career; his time was undoubtedly well spent.

In stylistic terms the house is an impressive example of his versatile use of the eclectic approach to architecture being carried out by his peers such as Vilaseca or Domènech. The *Casa Vicens* is a lyrical and confident demonstration of Gaudí's creative mastery of an Orientalist architectural style. The house originally was enclosed on one side by a neighbouring convent; despite this Gaudí has created an ornate oriental palace set in a garden adorned with an elaborate fountain. The oriental style was then very much in vogue across Europe, and it is also important to recall the Moorish contribution to Spanish architecture. Granada's Alhambra is the most famous of a number of buildings architects could look to. In addition many of the principles of Moorish design had become incorporated into house design, such as the use of materials like brick, tile and water to create decorative effects; all these were explored by Gaudí.

The top storey, with its brick columns dressed in green and white tiles leading up to the domed turrets, demonstrates Gaudí's use of Moorish architectural elements. However, his concern to create an exotic image of the oriental is not the product of methodical application of principles, but a creative elaboration of them. The arches on the ground floor and in the top storey clearly refer to the decorative arches found in Moorish architecture, however, Gaudí has moved away from simply imitating them. Instead he managed to evoke them through a more abstract geometric design. The patterned green and white tiles accentuate this geometric form. All of these early houses demonstrate Gaudí's inventiveness in his ability to develop architectural traditions in new and creative ways.

The elements of fantasy and pleasure so closely entwined with the artistic borrowing from the countries of Asia and Africa play an important role in this house. The domed turrets provide balconies to be reached by a rooftop walkway, and after surveying the garden with its palm trees, the owners could descend to the elaborate smoking room, which is a paradigmatic example of late nineteenth century Orientalist taste.

However, here the decorated vaulting again reveals another facet of Gaudí's inventiveness. To create this effect he has not relied on the traditional techniques of Moorish architects, but instead employed modern techniques – the tiles applied to the walls are reliefs made of compressed cardboard! This was made by another of Gaudí's clients Hermengildo Miralles Anglés. The tiles were originally coloured dark blue, and this colour scheme was taken up in the yellow and blue carnations painted in oil. The smoking room illustrates how Gaudí's skills encompassed not only the designs of a building's exterior, but also the creation of interior space and its decoration: Gaudí the designer is seen alongside the architect. His decorative skills are also apparent in the dining room with the doorways surrounded by images of birds and flowers bountifully flowing between the beams. The organic motifs are continued in brightly coloured relief along the walls. It has been proposed that Gaudí drew on images from an English magazine for these designs, which signals his interest in looking for developments beyond the traditions of his native Catalonia. Nonetheless the Mediterranean culture also exerts a strong presence. Four poetic inscriptions run around the room that correspond with the house's physical orientation to the position of the sun. For example in the south east, where the sun would reach in the morning, it reads 'Sol, solet, vina'm a veure que tinc fret' ('Sun, little sun, come and see me, I am feeling the cold').

It is important to establish early on that many of these rich, decorative features are evidence of the development of Gaudí's workshop. It is beyond the scope of this book to examine the role of Gaudí's assistants in detail for all his buildings, yet the contribution of his team of assistants needs always to be borne in mind. José Torrescassana Sellarés and Antonio Riba García worked on the painting and sculptures in the dining room respectively. A second sculptor who contributed was Lorenzo Matamala Pinyol, a childhood friend of Gaudí's, who would play a central role in the studio at the *Sagrada Familia*. He made a clay model of palm leaf, which Juan Oñós transformed into iron for the front gate. Seen as part of the façade this motif set the modernist and orientalist tone of the house, and also marks the first of a number of gates that Gaudí and his studio would create to set a dramatic opening cadence to the architectural experience of his houses. While the *Casa Vicens* was under construction Gaudí was working on his first rural house, known as *El Capricho*. It was commissioned in 1883 by don Máximo Díaz de Quijano. The building was completed by 1885 and the furniture and interior decoration finally concluded in 1887. There is debate amongst *Gaudinistas* as to whether Gaudí ever actually visited the site, Bassegoda i Nonell is of the opinion he did as there are many details that would have required his attention. However, what is certain is that the director of works was Cristóbal Cascante Colom, who used a maquette designed by Gaudí. The working relationship between Gaudí and Cascante had been established in school projects they had worked on together.

39. Casa Vicens, View of façade with window detail.
40. Casa Vicens, Window with moulded iron dragon.
41. Casa Vicens, Window with moulded iron dragon.

El Capricho

E l Capricho (the Caprice), as the name implies, was a rural retreat intended for pleasurable escapes from work and urban life. As pleasure was a key aspect of his brief, Gaudí created an imaginative solution that echoes many of the fantastic elements of the *Casa Vicens*; the two buildings are closely linked in a number of ways.

El Capricho makes evident Gaudí's eclecticism, which is characterised by confident use, not simple imitation, of architectural traditions and models. In this case the model is the medieval castle as is clearly evoked by the elaborate tower. Don Quijano would no doubt have enjoyed these romantic allusions to the medieval fiefdom, a welcome escape into the glories of the past from the realities of modern commercial life.

Gothic eclectic architecture is even more clearly alluded to in the pointed windows, and eclecticism is also evident in the contrast of the arabesque treatment of the tower and the portico with its classically inspired columns. It would not seem fanciful to suggest that one explanation for this choice of columns is necessity, as the tower is supported by them; a more elaborate Gothic system would have required a more complex solution.

Gaudí's ability to find creative solutions to architectural problems is signalled by his response to the unequal level of the site. The house has three floors. The entrance just mentioned opens onto the first floor, or what with regard to this elaborate type of house is known as the *planta nobile*.

Beneath this floor is a form of basement, which can be entered from the other side of the building. The rooms at this level included a kitchen, washing room and garage, while the floor above was for the principal inhabitants of the house, with the dining room, *salon* and a bedroom. The top floor added additional bedrooms but also access to the tower, the balcony at its base and a rooftop terrace.

The distinct levels of the house were demarcated by their materials. The ground floor, with rusticated stone blocks, provided a solid physical and visual foundation. On the west side where the ground is higher these foundations are only three blocks high. The white stone columns of the main entrance, clearly demarcating the principal floor of the house, offer a contrast to the walls, which are built of alternating red and yellow bricks divided by bands of ceramic tiles with leaves and sunflowers. The top floor is essentially an attic storey; the same ceramic tiles are used and they also dress the gabled windows which open through the sloping tiled roofs of the top floor.

The tower is dressed in the same ceramic tiles, and a spiral staircase leads up to a balcony surrounded by an elegant iron balustrade, which is crowned with

42. El Capricho, Tower.
43. El Capricho, Front facade.

the temple-like structure which seems to float on four fine columns. Similarities may be noted with the *Casa Vicens* in the use of ceramic tiles and the ironwork.

Unfortunately, due to reforms and repairs, the interior decoration has not been as well preserved as in the *Casa Vicens*. Nevertheless, further references to Islamic architecture remain, in niches designed for plants.

In addition to this aspect of Gaudí's work, it is important to mention his design for the garden, which included walls, a fountain and an artificial cave. These architectural elements he would develop in the Park Güell.

44. El Capricho, Main entrance.
45. El Capricho, North facade.
46. El Capricho, East facade.

Houses for Two Friends and a Painter

Before turning our attention to the final two houses that mark the culmination of Gaudí's domestic architecture it is worth noting a number of minor projects he undertook. Some are of a smaller scale and others were either never completed or else little evidence remains of them. Two projects that reveal Gaudí's capacity to work on small scale projects also show his willingness to work for friends.

In 1899 Gaudí designed a house for the painter Alejo Clapés Puig. It still stands today, and has the unusual distinction of having been overlooked until 1976, due its simplicity. For these reasons little further mention need be made of it here, except to acknowledge Clapés' contribution to the decoration in the *Palacio Güell* as well as in the house known as *La Pedrera*.

In 1900 Gaudí also undertook to reform the façade of the house of his close friend, the Dr. Pedro Santaló Castellví. Again there is very little in the final façade he designed that shows the remarkable skill apparent in the buildings discussed thus far. The principal significance of this work is his willingness to work on more modest projects for friends. The following year he was commissioned to decorate a Barcelona house of the Marquesa de Castelldosrius. He worked on the project for three years, but no record exists of the fruits of his labour, as it was destroyed during the Spanish Civil War. On completion of this project Gaudí began designs for a chalet for the painter Luis Graner that was never finished.

However, there are two tantalising pieces of evidence that indicate the new direction of Gaudí's architectural ideas. A small sketch of the planned house suggests a transformation of the *Bellesguard* design, with its tall tower, but the bulky volume of the rural house has been replaced by a more organically formed exterior, with a greater emphasis on curved lines.

Apart from the foundations the only other evidence we have of the building is the gateway. After his student design for a cemetery gate and the entrance to the *Casa Vicens* Gaudí went on to design a number of imaginative and inspiring entrances and gateways. Some of his most famous were for Eusebio Güell and are examined below. In anticipation of this later examination a brief comment should be made about the gate way for Graner's chalet. It is evidence of a playful dimension to Gaudí's thinking. The principal entrance of the gateway is for vehicles, and to one side there is a small doorway for pedestrians, however, above this is a small round opening, which Gaudí called the 'the little birds' gate'. The profile of this stone gateway indicates a similar design to the sketch of the house with bold curving forms.

Casa Batlló

Another small scale project in which Gaudí was involved is known as the *Torre Damian Mateu*. The building is actually attributed to the architect Francesc Berenguer Mestres, who worked as an assistant to Gaudí.

The most likely reason Gaudí left this project to his assistant is that in 1906, when the contract was drawn up, he was fully immersed in his penultimate large scale residential project, the *Casa Batlló*. The signs of change seen in the traces of what the Chalet Graner may have become are fully evident in the last two houses Gaudí worked on.

In a sense, to name them houses is to misname them; they are like the *Casa de los Botines* or *Casa Calvet*, like large apartment buildings. Gaudí's involvement with the first of these, the *Casa Batlló*, began in 1904 as a work of restoration. There were three specific tasks required for the reform: a redesign of the façade; widening of the interior patio; and rearrangement of the room distribution, particularly of the principal apartment, belonging to Señor Batlló. It is perhaps more appropriate to use the word transformation given the appearance of the building when work finished in 1906.

The façade provides a dramatic indication of the development of Gaudí's thinking. The solid stone columns of the ground floor provide a series of cavernous openings, shaded by an undulating overhang which supports the columns for the windows of the first floor, or *piano nobile* apartment. Here Gaudí formed the stone into a fluid, shifting form. No longer is Gaudí working in an eclectic manner with a recognisable architectural vocabulary, instead the structure seems derived from the study of natural and organic substances. The first floor windows appear supported by sinewy and bonelike structure.

However, the slender columns which divide the windows may be seen as a development of the slender columns of the Gothic windows of *Bellesguard* in the sense of the weightlessness they create. The sculptural solidity of the first two floors gradually gives way to a less weighty arrangement of balconies and windows arranged across a coloured surface scored with discs.

In the transition from the first to the second floor, the task of the reform is evident. The dramatic forms of the ground and first floors, which culminate in the far side windows of the second floor and the two balconies they create on the third floor, have been essentially grafted onto the building.

63. Casa Batlló, View of top floors and roof.

First Church Designs

An account of Gaudí's early religious work continues to be a catalogue of the losses caused by anti-clerical attacks during Spain's Civil war. In 1882 Gaudí was commissioned to build a church in the town of Villaricos in Alemería, a region in southern Spain. The church, dedicated to the Holy Spirit, was planned to accompany the establishment of a new monastery for the order of St. Benedict.

Gaudí delivered a plan for a neo-Gothic church after four months. The project never proceeded beyond this planning stage, and knowledge of what Gaudí had set to paper was lost in the fire at the *Sagrada Familia*.

Nonetheless it has been argued that an idea of the building may be gleaned from the final form of a different church known as *Las Salesas*.

Gaudí worked on this church with his teacher Martorell, with whom he worked closely on a number of other projects at this time, such as the College Church for the Jesuits in Barcelona.

The combined use of brick, stone and ceramics at *Las Salesas* suggests Gaudí may have intended to use the same materials he had begun experimenting with in his domestic buildings like the *Casa Vicens* and *El Capricho*.

Furthermore it is interesting to note that it was during this period that he established relationships with a number of important craftsmen, including the metalworker Juan Oños, the glassmaker Amigó, the sculptor Juan Flotats and the mosaic designer Luigi Pallarin.

A New Façade for Barcelona's Cathedral

Collaboration was at the root of another project that we do have clear evidence of, which is a design for a new façade for the Cathedral of Barcelona. The façade had never been completed since the work on the cathedral itself was finished in the fifteenth-century. Following a somewhat complex process of canvassing ideas for the new façade, an exhibition was held in 1882 of the proposals which had been collected. The exhibition consisted of works by Manuel Girona, José Oriol Mestres and Juan Martorell. The results were divisive, with all the newspapers engaging in the debate and either vehemently criticising or ardently supporting different candidates.

The project appealed to the public sensibility as it became a symbolic focus for a physical expression of Barcelona's present reviving the glories of the past. The final decision favouring the collaborative project of Mestres and Augusto Font Carreras would not be taken until in 1887, and in the meantime debate raged. Gaudí's support lay with Martorell, his teacher and with whom he was then working. He was not alone in holding this position.

In 1882 he was one of twenty eight Barcelona architects who signed a document supporting Martorell. With his commitment to restoring Catalonia's heritage Gaudí's backing was strong and followed by action. He assisted with the design for the 1882 exhibition.

Five years later, in 1887, he reproduced the same design, with assistance from Dòmenech i Montaner for publication in the journal *la Renaixença*. The design reveals the powerful hold of the Gothic style on Barcelona's architects. Although the design was not Gaudí's his involvement in the planning of a project on this scale would have provided him with a valuable experience that he would be able to draw on when designing the façades of the *Sagrada Familia*, which he was soon to undertake.

Martorell's design was criticised in 1882 by one of the newspapers for departing from Catalan Gothic and becoming too Germanic in its appearance. In some ways this concords with Robert Hughes analysis of Catalan Gothic as being much plainer than many of the styles developed in France, Germany and Britain.

Hence it may be suggested that Martorell's study of these non-Catalan forms, particularly the emphasis given to a soaring verticality and the use of sculpture, may have prompted Gaudí to think along similar lines in the lengthy evolution of his design for the *Sagrada Familia*; although this process would lead Gaudí to the development of bold original approaches to the design and decoration of a cathedral.

77. Design for Facade of Cathedral of Barcelona.

Two Altarpieces

The year following the exhibition of designs for the cathedral façade, when work began on Gaudí's Orientalist *Casa Vicens*, he also designed a chapel dedicated to the Holy Sacrament for the parish church of San Félix de Aella. The project received approval but was never brought to fruition. The existence of a design offers a valuable idea of Gaudí's intentions. The design suggests a restrained use of architectural elements, with the decorative features focused on the design of the altarpiece. Rising above the tabernacle he planned to show Christ on the cross with the Virgin and St. John at its base. The rays of light, which Gaudí would no doubt have gilded or coloured, fan out to the sculptured mandala form with the row of cherubs along its edge. Around this dramatic visual focus at the centre of the altarpiece the treatment of the altar combines painted decorations of the word "*sanctus*" and Gothic patterns. It is crowned by an arcade of pointed arches and a row of trefoils, above which rise angels and a second cross, this time signifying Christ's resurrection. Bassegoda Nonnell has discussed how this arrangement is far more than decorative; like Gaudí's design for a cemetery gate it is based on a close reading of the book of revelation of St. John the Evangelist. For example the seven angels planned for the stained glass of the windows are a direct reference to this divine text. Gaudí's meticulous attention to detail was not simply a result of his interests in the aesthetic appearance of his architecture, but underpinned by a concern that the building should express a deeper spiritual significance.

In 1885 Gaudí began work on another altarpiece, although this time it was much smaller in scale, measuring only 176 x 85 x 9 centimetres. However, it does exist and it provides an opportunity to examine a Gaudí design in wood rather than stone or metal. The mahogany wood altar is varnished and its dark colour enhanced by the use of gilded decoration in the *predella*. Although working on this small scale, Gaudí has incorporated architectural elements such as the columns, with sculpted cherubs, carved floral motifs as well as images and sacred text. The carpenter Federico Laboria was responsible for actually building the work. Laboria also worked with Gaudí on the *Sagrada Familia*.

Representing Ecclesiastical Authority: the Bishop's Palace, Astorga

As mentioned above Gaudí was known to Bishop Grau. On the sixteenth of October 1886 he became Bishop of Astorga. Just over two months later a fire destroyed the Bishop's palace.

However, the unfortunate events that were to begin the Bishop's governance of the diocese were to lead to an important contract for Gaudí, and the construction of another of his few buildings located outside Barcelona.

At first the Church administration examined the option of contracting a local architect, but there was nobody capable of carrying out the work. It was at this point that Bishop Grau thought of Gaudí, having then recently carried out the ceremony to consecrate Gaudí's chapel for the nuns of *Jesús y María*.

By the end of February 1887 the committee responsible for building the new cathedral had a positive answer from Gaudí, a request for information about the project and an explanation that he could not come to Astorga until he had finished the work on the Barcelona palace for Eusebio Güell.

The projects that were mounting up for Gaudí during this time combined with Astorga's distance from Barcelona posed complications for his work on the palace, which was not actually finished until 1960! A catalogue of difficulties interfered with the project up until this date. With regard to Gaudí's life the principal problem arose with the death of Bishop Grau in September 1893, four years after work began. Gaudí designed a catafalque for his funeral, now lost, as well as his tombstone.

However, his commitment to his patron could not keep the project underway. The Diocesan council halted it and serious problems arose between them and Gaudí. A letter from Gaudí in 1892 reveals that Gaudí was not being paid on time, and he complains that in contrast to private patrons the state had no sense of treating people with dignity and justice. In any case Gaudí resigned on the 4ᵗ of November 1893.

78. Episcopal Palace of Astorga, View from behind.

However, it would seem that Gaudí's resignation was given under pressure. Some years later the Princess Isabel de Borbon asked him why he had neglected this work and he replied that he did not leave but was fired! As a result of this conversation with the princess, Gaudí was given a posthumous declaration of gratitude from the state, dated 1894.

Despite Gaudí's early retirement from the building work his plans have been carried out and the building remains an impelling example of a modern response to the Gothic style.

As an institutional commission the planning stages of the Bishop's Palace were lengthy. The official approval was given on the 20th of February in 1889, after the plans had been passed between a Diocese council, the Ministry of Grace and Justice and the Royal Academy of Fine Arts of San Fernando in Madrid, as well as Gaudí and the Bishop. Hoping to avoid past experiences one of the Academy's specifications was for Gaudí to ensure that the woodwork was protected from risk of fire.

Besides Gaudí's designs two recorded exchanges between him and the Bishop offer a valuable insight into his ideas for this building. One is extremely practical. The bishop reminded Gaudí not to overlook the cold winters of Astorga and to include a central heating system. Although pleased with Gaudí's design of a grand building in the Gothic style the Bishop was keen for it to include the comforts of modern technology.

Gaudí's response reveals his understanding of the structural issues that accompanied the installation of such modern advances. He stated that central heating must be accompanied by good ventilation or else it becomes unhealthy.

In the second exchange between architect and bishop, Grau suggested the use of artificial stone, which Gaudí rejected on the basis that this was only appropriate for buildings of secondary importance; Gaudí was clearly planning to build a work that upheld the status of the bishop.

Although Gaudí was always prepared to experiment with the most humble materials, such as cardboard in the *Casa Vicens* or broken plates in the Güell

Park, in this work he sought to maintain a sense of architectural decorum. A bishop's palace, like the Güell Palace for example, should reflect the status of its inhabitants. Gaudí's work in Astorga undoubtedly creates a sense of Episcopal authority.

The expression of ecclesiastical status at the Astorga Episcopal palace is commanded through a bold, monumental rendering of the Gothic style. The size of the rooms shown on the floor plan and the dramatic impressions created by the façade clearly demonstrate this.

Gaudí combined forms reminiscent of Church architecture with those of the medieval fortress; the palace is surrounded by a moat. It may be assumed that Gaudí's design, perhaps following request of the bishop and the diocese, was for the palace to match the late Gothic style of the city's cathedral.

With regard to the fortress appearance it is worth remembering that up until the mid-fifteenth century bishops frequently commanded small armies and combined their spiritual role with the defence of the temporal realm under their administration.

An important significance of this project is that not only was Gaudí able to explore his interest in the medieval architectural heritage, but he was restricted to a more conservative brief.

Within the restrictions of this brief he demonstrated his understanding of the principles of the Gothic as well as incorporating original and modern elements into the design.

Gaudí's abilities as an architect are apparent not only in his grand visionary projects but also in the subtlety of his more restrained projects.

The palace is built entirely of granite, and the light colour of this resilient stone offsets the undressed stonework; as in his other buildings Gaudí maintained a balance between monumental weight and a sense of grace. The numerous groups of windows are central to this and they add a strong vertical emphasis to the building.

79. Episcopal Palace of Astorga, Chimney.
80. Episcopal Palace of Astorga, View of entrance.
81. Episcopal Palace of Astorga, Entrance porch detail.
82. Episcopal Palace of Astorga, General view.